Reflective Haiku:
Poems for Growing, Healing, and Restoring the Soul

S3B

Praise for Reflective Haiku:
Poems for Growing, Healing, and Restoring the Soul

I can't tell U how much I enjoyed reading this book. The well-crafted thought process; the progression of work from the 1st 2 the last poem; the insightful, uplifting messages that span the entire book, the sheer weight of each piece... I honestly can't say enough. I was genuinely moved by the 1st poem. The "Living With Grief" section particularly hits hard but stands as a guide 2 bring the reader through their own grief by embracing it as a mere aspect of the fullness of life. She then uses the next 2 chapters, "Letting Go" and "Joy," to logically lead the reader out of grief as part of the process. It's beautiful. S3B displays a lifetime of earned wisdom. She is a gifted gardener sowing seeds N2 the souls of what I expect 2 B millions of readers. This brilliant body of work is bound 2 save someone's life, and it feels as if it was meant 2 B that way.

Khari B.[1]
author, educator, spoken word musician

---

[1] Khari B. is known for his mix of standard and non-standard English when sharing thoughts through writing.

It's hard not to want to read a book with the title *Reflective Haiku: Poems for Growing, Healing, and Restoring the Soul*. Who among us doesn't want to grow, to heal, to restore our soul? Dr. Barnes sets a big order for her haiku with a title like that. The good news is that she delivers. I appreciate that she takes haiku seriously. She understands its history and doesn't dismiss what the original form can actually accomplish, and she is careful to make sure her readers do, also. Yet she is also able to use the form to deliver her sincere thoughts on ways to grow, heal and restore the soul. This book makes a wonderful gift for yourself and those you love. It's fun and insightful, as it uses the compact and powerful tool of the haiku form as a resource for a fulfilling life.

Joyce Brinkman
Indiana's first poet laureate, 2002-2008
Co-author, Seasons of Sharing A Kasen Renku Collaboration

Brave Brothers Books LLC
1389 W. 86th Street #186
Indianapolis, IN 46260
www.bravebrothersbooks.com

Reflective Haiku: Poems for Growing, Healing, and Restoring the Soul

Copyright © 2020 by S3B

Twitter@BraveBrosBooks

All rights reserved. No part of this book may be used or reproduced by any means, graphic, electronic, or mechanical, including photocopying, recording, taping or by any information storage retrieval system without the written permission of the publisher except in the case of brief quotations embodied in articles and reviews.

Editor: Christine Egner
Cover & Interior Design: Suzanne Parada

Library of Congress Control Number: 2023910795

Published August 2023 in the United States by
Brave Brothers Books, LLC
ISBN 13: 978-1-952099-04-5

Dedications

To My Heavenly Father
Thank you for my life
For blessings, including a
mind to learn and love

To My Teacher
Khari B., our
Discopoet flipped the switch
a writer was born

To My Husband, Jermaine
champions my feats
I won't ever not need him
forever side guide

To My Son, Jerry
sarcastic, like me
our humor–mirror image
laughter echoes on

To My Son, James
accomplished artist
dedicated creative
expression master

To My Dad
confidence builder
unshakeable supporter
model for my life

Table of Contents

Introduction VIII

Choice at the Fork 1

Towards Another Sunrise 5

Pushing Through 9

Living with Loss 13

Letting Go 17

Joy 21

Vows to Me 25

The Seeds We Plant 29

About the Author 32

About the Illustrator 33

About the Colorist 34

Introduction

Haiku is a Japanese poetry form consisting of three lines. The first and third lines contain only five syllables, and the second has seven. In the traditional form, haiku poems focus on nature and the natural world and zoom in on a moment. A reference to a season through sensory language is quite common in the traditional form.

As a former middle and high school English teacher and elementary and high school literacy coach, I always emphasized the importance of making poetry your own and breaking the rules.

In modern haiku, the topic does not always center on nature, sensory language may not be prevalent, and the 5-7-5 syllable count is not always followed.

When I was in college at Purdue University, I joined one of the Black Cultural Center (BCC) performing arts ensembles, the Haraka Writers. This group wrote and performed poetry. One day, we were challenged to write a haiku that described us or an aspect of ourselves. I wrote:

> *my bluntness might sting,*
> *but I will not hold it in*
> *to keep you from tears*

This haiku was later published in one of the BCC's newsletters. That haiku still resonates with me to this day because that haiku allowed me to convey a message in a few words. It prevented me from providing too much context and background before saying what I wanted to say.

With that thought in mind, I wrote this poetry book which is divided into eight chapters. Each chapter contains ten haiku. The poems follow the 5-7-5 pattern, but other traditional elements of haiku are not included in all poems.

One more thing... Just like "sheep" is the singular and plural form, "haiku" is the singular and plural form. Students always ask, so I thought I would include that tiny tidbit.

Let's get to reading!

Enjoy!

S3B

CHOICE AT THE FORK

1 | **Show Up**
doubt, but don't dip out
fears become reality
when you're a no-show

2 | **Indecision is a Decision**
neutral space between
decision, indecision
be bold; choose something

3 | **Choose to Improve**
it is will or skill
or both, but it's idleness
to address neither

4 | **Part of the Process**
losing self-control
and finding yourself are just
different sides, same coin

5 | **Boil**
liquid H2O
212° unstable
you water or gas?

---

[2] Water boils at 212 degrees and transforms from a liquid to a gas (water vapor).

6 | Free?

you cannot expect
freedom from anyone else
when you have the key

7 | It Might Stink, But

don't hate manure
fertilizer aids the growth
endure it and bloom

8 | Stay or Go?

if the road's not straight,
will you stay or venture forth...
to discover more?

9 | Your Tools

tools for victory
tools for a catastrophe
jailed in your body

10 | Fight the Fear

the fear of failure
an anchor lodged in the sea
lift it and set sail

TOWARDS ANOTHER SUNRISE

11 | **; not .**

    tomorrow's sunrise
    is a horizon of hope
    be here to see it

12 | **Shade & Shine**

    shade brings no comfort
    greatness wants to shine, but you
    must leave the shadows

13 | **Bend, Don't Break**

    think of mighty palms
    storms brutally attack them
    yet they lean, withstand

14 | **Smile Spreader**[3]

    spread smiles and give joy
    do not forget to save some
    for your heart's delight

15 | **Keep Your Streak**

    If you want to quit,
    know that your survival rate,
    so far, is perfect

---

[3] This poem was inspired by Stephen "tWitch" Boss' tweet on October 14, 2022, before he lost his life to suicide on December 14, 2022. The title comes from his IG bio, where he listed himself as a Smile Spreader.

16 | **The Framing**

Looking for defects?
You'll find them. Are they defects?
Depends on your lens.

17 | **Brick by Brick**

drowning with hatred
take critics' bricks; build your throne
center your intent

18 | **Broken Crayons Still Write**

burned, broken, and torn
battered, bruised, and discouraged,
yet still in the fight

19 | **Examination**

blinded by sunlight
curtains pulled back; truth exposed
extinguish demons

20 | **An Anchor**

we must part with flesh
parting early is tempting
reach for a tether

PUSHING THROUGH

21 | **Thrive**
　press on and push back
　your existence is protest
　you deserve to thrive

22 | **Self-Validation**
　it doesn't matter
　if it doesn't matter if
　it matters to you

23 | **270 Degrees**[4]
　look back like an owl
　feet gripped down, facing forward
　whip head 'round and soar

24 | **Battle Cry**[5]
　from deep within, yell
　aaaaaaaaah! living's a battle cry
　live glass shattering

25 | **Get to the Goal**
　where others halted
　press right on past them; get what
　they failed to obtain

---
[4] Owls can rotate their heads 270 degrees.
[5] Dedicated to Discopoet Khari B., facilitator of Purdue University's Black Cultural Center's Haraka Writers Ensemble. Khari had his writers yell before and after each poetry session and performance.

26 | Pressure
apply the pressure
consistently with vigor
please let them flinch first

27 | Assured
when no one can change
your mind, be assured that you
can commit this time

28 | Do It Scared, But...
predicted failures
become reality when
scared and unprepared

29 | The Fear Flow
face flushed with fever
jumpy stomach, tense muscles
fearfully push through

30 | Nothing But Jealousy
the haters talk trash
about your life because their
life is so boring

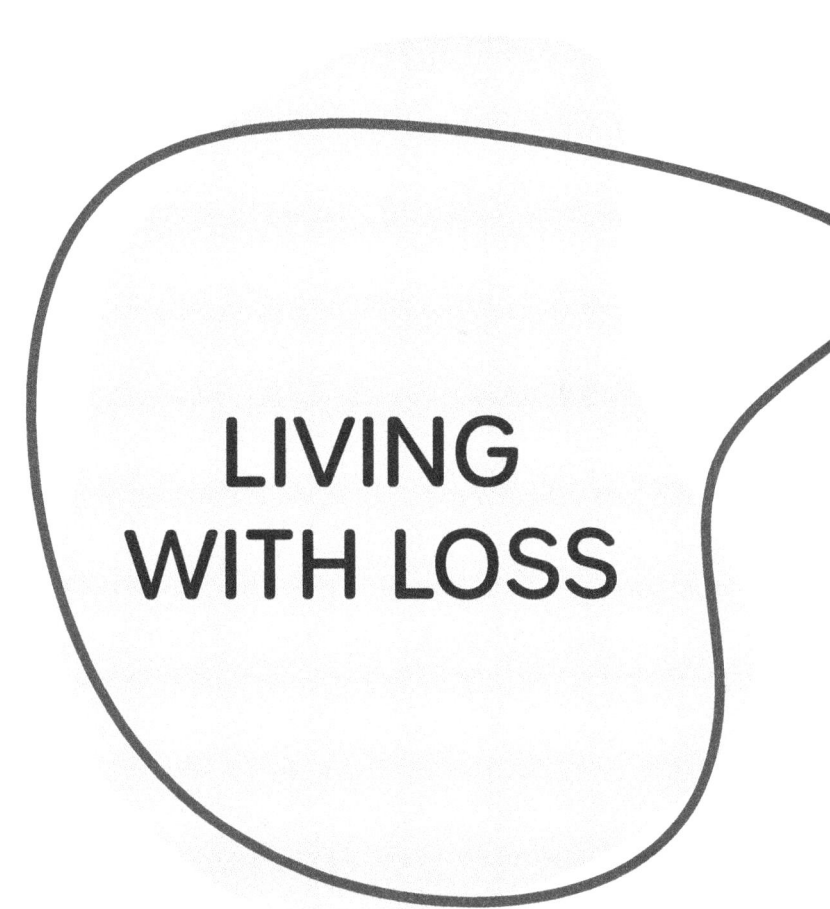

LIVING WITH LOSS

31 | **Grief**

inhaling deeply
before the complete exhale
a blow to the ribs

32 | **Beyond Sympathy**

not your sympathy
only your understanding
no more canned comments

33 | **Grief & Love**

grief is your trapped love
yearning to make deposit
great love leaves great pain

34 | **Grace**

enveloped in warmth
like a July summer day
love's gentle hug, grace

35 | **Silent Love**

no words, no gifts, and
no way to make it right – just
silence side by side

36 | **Grief & Love II**

the sorrows of the
tomorrows without you show
the power of love

37 | **Find Your Moon**

choose moon over sun
sun illuminates bright days
moon, light in darkness

38 | **Never Gone**

a floating fragrance
tears flow into waterfalls
the love lingers on

39 | **Grief II**

inescapable
stuck like skin wrapped around bones
grief, a life partner

40 | **The Waves**

waves ebb and flow; I,
caught in between, sometimes seek
dry land to find peace

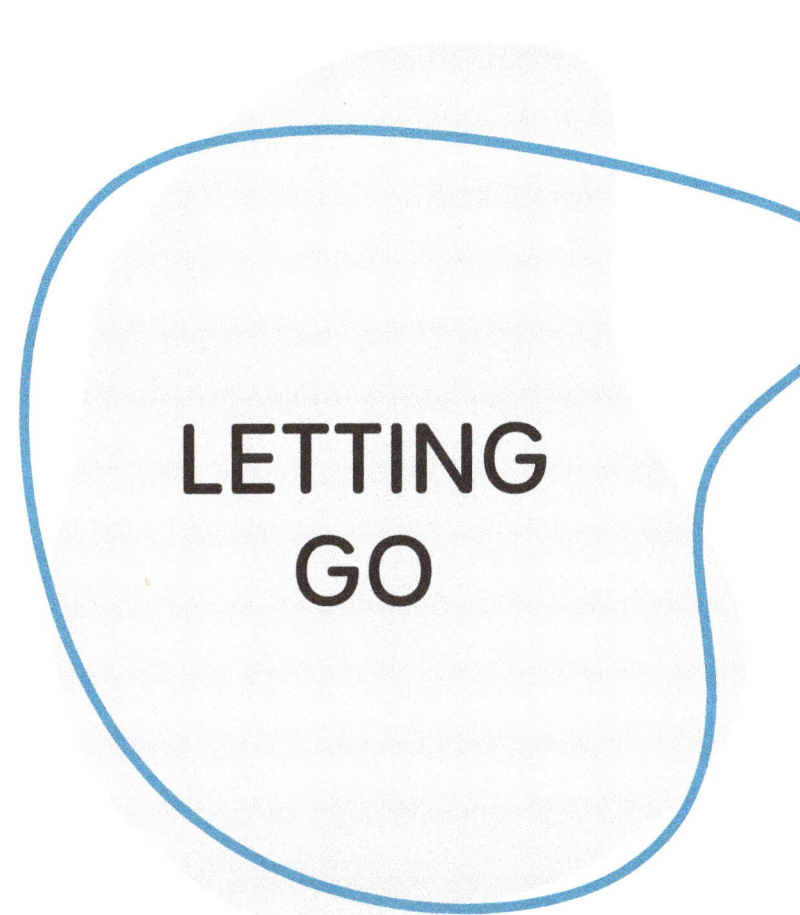

LETTING GO

41 | **Blow & Let It Go**

deep breath in, and hold.
release. blow. relax shoulders.
release the tension.

42 | **Drop the Mask**

"Hello! How are you?"
"I'm doing fine." <sigh> "Real talk,
I could be better..."

43 | **Let It Flow Away**

laughter can block tears
why laugh to keep from crying?
let it wash away

44 | **Goodbye Explanations**

"Demand me nothing."[6]
Are you satisfied? If so,
release explaining

45 | **Farewell For Now**

goodbye. no. good. bye.
bye is hard but a good. bye.
means see you later

---

[6] This line is from Shakespeare's *Othello*. The character Iago says this line instead of explaining his actions.

46 | Beyond This
> rudderless stardust
> unknown siren call beckons
> a journey beyond

47 | Sip & Cry
> sip of aged bourbon
> adrift in distant gazing
> pity for short while

48 | Can't Come to the Phone
> ignored texts and calls
> bonnet, blanket, book, and bed
> rest is resistance

49 | Shed Skin
> like the shed snake skin
> a new exoskeleton
> a fresh beginning

50 | Held Breath
> like Bernadine's[7] hair
> like the match she lit and dropped
> cut. burn. exhale. leave.

---

[7] Bernadine Harris is a fictional character in the book *Waiting to Exhale* by Terry McMillan. Two popular scenes in the movie (of the same name) are when Bernadine cuts her long hair and when she sets fire to a car with her husband's belongings in it after she learns he had an affair.

51 | **Tickled**

tickled belly laughs
spreading contagious delight
bring on more of this

52 | **Seasons of Joy**

winter comes for all
before the cold, bloom in spring
dance in the summer

53 | **Freedom to Be**

fulfill your desires
you owe no explanations
emancipation

54 | **An Action Word**

sing, run, dance, eat, walk,
gaze, kiss, hug, read … do something
joy is an action

55 | **Joy of Missing Out**

avoid burnout's grasp
find bliss in JOMO's retreat
selective delight

56 | **A Way with Words**

    textual passion
    Logophile's mind ignites fire
    wild brain in motion

57 | **Chasing Joy**

    like a child dropping
    toys to chase a firefly
    pursue happiness

58 | **Skin**

    return to Eden
    wrapped in nothing but raindrops
    birthday suit freedom

59 | **The Blacker the Berry...**

    the sweeter the juice
    darker & deeper the roots
    greater is the fruit

60 | **Powerful Words**

    pen and page collide
    definitely mightier
    transformative force

VOWS TO ME

61 | **Love You**

> will you love, comfort,
> honor, keep in sickness? health?
> convince the mirror

62 | **Crown**

> chin to chest, it slips
> chin up. back straight. shoulders down.
> recenter your crown

63 | **Too Much**

> if I am too much
> find less — I keep expanding
> never fit boxes

64 | **Let It Burn**

> burning bridges down
> prevents backtracking mistakes
> freedom, new path found

65 | **Leap**

> no waiting for signs
> leap like a bungee jumper
> face what you avoid

66 | Clearance[8]
value recognized
no need for clearance or sales
confidence in worth

67 | Taxes
value understood
tax added without remorse
true worth reflected

68 | No Explanation Needed
Bobby B told us
"It's my prerogative,"[9] so
no compromising

69 | Why Copy and Paste?
screenshot, copy, screen-
shot, copy, image blurs. be
clear, not a copy

70 | Move to Your Music
heart, the drummer's beat
brain, composition writer
body, feet mover

---

[8] Inspired by Pastor John F. Ramsey's sermon "Identity Theft: Stolen Identity."
[9] "It's My Prerogative" was a hit song on Bobby Brown's album, *Don't Be Cruel.*

THE SEEDS WE PLANT

71 | **Two Hands**

one hand reaches up
the other hand reaches back
this won't make you lack

72 | **Legacy I**

one day, you will bolt[10]
will your seeds multiply, or
just shrivel and die?

73 | **Legacy II**

work done for you lives,
dies with you, but for others
it lives beyond you

74 | **Pass the Light**

as a sparkler's light
dims down, before fading, it
can light another

75 | **I do. We do. You do.**

it's I, we, you do
a teacher's lesson lives far
beyond teacher's life

---

[10] Bolting is when a plant flowers and goes to seed, signaling the end of the plant's life.

76 | **From Failure to Lesson**
don't hide your failures
allow your life lessons to
be someone's guidebook

77 | **Story Time**
sit by elder's feet
knowledge falls like shooting stars
oral history

78 | **When Time Runs Out**
hourglass sand dash
need 25-hour days
progeny flips glass

79 | **Yin & Yang: Teaching & Learning**
the teacher teaches
the learner learns, does the work
the learner teaches

80 | **In Due Season**[11]
don't lose heart or faith
parents, children, grands will reap
sow with persistence

---
[11] Inspired by Galatians 6:9 & Proverbs 13:22.

About the Author

Writer S3B
Shawnta Shicole Stockton Barnes
loves writing poems

called to educate
destined to survive and thrive
lover of learning

loving husband and
identical twin boys are
her joy and her world

in her spare time, she
finds serenity in her food
and flower garden

About the Illustrator

Artist James J. Barnes
is a middle school student
who lives in Indy

a published author
of mystery book Ghost Text,
written at 7

loves twin bro Jerry
in his spare time, James enjoys
illustrating for fun

About the Colorist

Digital artist,
Amanda Middleton is
a mother of two

Her art passion bloomed
during the pandemic, and
her talent was clear.

Dedicated to
her craft, she brings writer's words
alive through her art

References

Bloudoff-Indelicato, M. (2013). *How owls twist their heads almost 360 degrees*. National Geographic. https://www.nationalgeographic.com/animals/article/how-owls-twist-heads-almost-360-degrees#

Boss, S. [@offical_tWitch]. (2022). *Just a thought One of my favorite parts of flying on a cloudy day is when the plane breaks through* [Tweet]. Twitter. https://twitter.com/official_tWitch/status/1580988307969753088?s=20&t=UC8AHzgZvKfJsDoWqWZmow

Holy Bible, King James Version (2008). YouVersion. https://www.bible.com/bible/1/GAL.6.KJV

Holy Bible, King James Version (2008). YouVersion. https://www.bible.com/bible/1/PRO. 13.KJV

Italie, H. (1989). *Bobby Brown takes his prerogative, solo.* The Hour. https://news.google.com/news papers?id=lyIiAAAAIBAJ&pg=3447,293919

Kaufman, A. (2022). *At what temperature does water boil? Explaining water's boiling point and how long it will take.* USA TODAY. https://www.usatoday.com/story/life/food-dining/2022/07/19/at-what-temperature-does-water-boil/10088297002/

MasterClass. (2020). *6 ways to prevent vegetables from bolting.* https://www.masterclass.com/articles/ways-to-prevent-vegetables-from-bolting

Ramsey, J.F. (2022). *Identity Theft: Stolen Identity* [Sermon]. New Life Worship Center, Indianapolis, Indiana. https://www.facebook.com/nlwcindy/videos/818235982814441

Shakespeare, W. (1997). *The Tragedy of Othello, The Moor of Venice* (S. Greenblatt, W. Cohen, J.E. Howard, K. Eisaman Maus, Eds.). (W.W. Norton & Company, Inc.). (Original work published 1603-4)

www.ingramcontent.com/pod-product-compliance
Lightning Source LLC
Chambersburg PA
CBHW041133110526
44592CB00020B/2790